EXPAT ETIQUETTE

HOW TO LOOK GOOD IN BAD PLACES

MICHAEL BEAR & LIZ GOOD

NORTIA
PRESS

2321 E. 4th St., C-219
Santa Ana, CA 92705
USA

Expat Etiquette: How To Look Good in Bad Places.

ISBN: 978-1-940503-10-3
Library of Congress Control Number: 2015941752

Printed in the United States of America

Michael Bear:
To Lizzy Bear, who brings me home

Liz Good:
To all the many people who have helped me make
homes away from home

Not to share in the activity and passion of your time is to count as not having lived. I don't claim virtue. I claim a low level of boredom.

—William Sloan Coffin

As a student of disaster, I note that we react alike to our tribulations: frayed and bitter at the time, proud afterwards. Nothing is better for self-esteem than survival.

—Martha Gellhorn

CONTENTS.

Going overseas is hard. Leaving friends and family behind. Traveling to a country where you probably don't speak the language, and definitely don't understand the culture. Foreign foods, foreign diseases. Loneliness.

Of course, it does have its compensations. Smoking. Casual sex. Functional alcoholism. Add a little danger and excitement, and it's a difficult offer to refuse.

The physical act of going overseas is simple enough. Have ticket, will travel. Yet arrival alone doesn't confer any knowledge, let alone status. This book is a humble guide to all of those who not only want to travel to far away and sometimes dangerous lands—for the best or worst of reasons—but also want to do so with a modicum of style. Style defined as, "appearing to know what you're doing, even when you have no idea what's happening around you."

Because it's true, we all do look and act alike. The American, European, and antipodean travelers and expats. From Afghanistan to Zimbabwe, there's a distinct expatriate culture, a distinct lingo, a distinct way of dressing. It's about broadcasting your experience without resorting to native dress. It's about talking in place-names and acronyms.

It's about learning to use a squat toilet. And yes, you will use a squat toilet.

Having picked up a few tricks of the trade, we thought we'd put together a collection of best practices and lessons learned. Standard operating procedures, if you will, for navigating through some of the best and the worst places in the world.

Thus, we offer this sometimes-serious, some-times-tongue-in-cheek handbook on expat etiquette. Enjoy.

Cheers,
Michael and Liz

A Note on Semantics:
Who Is an Expat, Anyway?

The Merriam Webster dictionary defines an expatriate as, "a person who lives in a foreign country." Technically, a semester in Barcelona or a second home in Costa Rica might qualify. We take a somewhat more narrow view. This book is not, alas, written with the summer student or the sunshine tourist in mind. Instead, our travelers and expatriates are those brave and foolhardy souls who go overseas to places that don't tend to feature as tourist destinations. Places where the local color is a wee bit too colorful.

There's no set residency requirement, none of that posturing about the need to spend at least six months or a year or a decade in a country before you finally "begin to understand." We'll never truly understand. That's not so much an affirmation of ignorance as it is recognition of our limitations. Our tribe is, by definition, a nomadic one. Six months there, a year here, another two years there. It's about movement, a certain style and a certain state of mind.

GETTING THERE AND AWAY AND BACK AGAIN: TRAVELING TO PARTS LESS-KNOWN

The most important rule of thumb is that maps lie. They give the impression that a mile in the eastern Congo is the equivalent of a mile in the United States or in Europe. Yet distance is not just a function of space, or how far apart two places might be.

Instead, the only distance that really matters is that determined by a function of time, or how long it takes to get from one point to another.

You can get from New York to San Francisco in about six hours. In eastern Congo or South Sudan it might take that long to go forty miles. If you're lucky.

Nonexistent roads, washed out bridges, planes flown by drunken Russians. In reality, the Congo is almost infinitely large, while the US or Europe are relatively small.

What to Pack

There are certain travelers who've reached a stage of packing nirvana, where they're able to fit everything they could ever need into a small carry-on bag. Envy and fear those people.

For the rest of us, we know we should pack as little as possible, but often "as little as possible" always seems to (a) be too much, and (b) leave out certain essentials.

To that end, the absolutely essential packing list should include:

1. Electrical outlet adapters. Extra points if you're ever in a country that uses the diagonal pronged adaptors.

2. Gatorade packets, energy bars, and immodium, for the inevitable bout of dysentery.

3. Cheap sunglasses.

4. Contact lens solution. Unless, that is, you're

happy navigating the world nearly blind. A backup pair of glasses is also useful.

5. Sunscreen.

6. Tampons, tampons, tampons. You really don't want to be left without should the need arise.

7. Condoms.

8. A portable French press—that is, if you like coffee and you plan to stay in your new destination a while.

9. A flashlight or a headtorch. Because the only thing worse than a latrine at night is a dark latrine at night.

Things You Think You'll Need But Won't Ever Use

1. Heavy-duty super-fancy rain gear. If you're out and about during the rainy season, you'll almost always be in a building or a car. If you get caught in a monsoon; you're going to get wet no matter what.

2. Clothing that seems appropriate to the context, but that you'd never wear in the West. If you don't like that wrinkly linen shirt in Oslo, chances are you still won't like it when you get to South Sudan.

3. Anything that could be described as "native dress." Because, no matter what you wear, you won't blend in, though you will look ridiculous trying to do so.

4. A fancy dress and high-heeled shoes. If the need does materialize, you can get 'em there. A suit is also usually unnecessary, unless you plan to spend a lot of time hobnobbing with government ministers.

Other Words of Semi-Wisdom

Check your visa before you travel. Ditto with yellow fever card. Seriously. It's shocking how often these details get overlooked, and often with expensive repercussions.

Be sure your earplugs and facemask are in your carry-on; they're the only way you might actually catch some shut-eye on that overnight transcontinental flight. Well, unless you manage to score some prescription meds from your friendly neighborhood doctor. We recommend Ambien, but Xanax works too.

A note on luggage—you want to choose bags that don't in any way advertise your relative wealth, or the value of the various clothing and electronic goods inside. So, best to leave the Louis Vuitton travel bag in the closet. Instead, use old, well-worn, sturdy luggage. The only problem is that many other people have roughly the same idea, meaning it can be hard to distinguish your bag when it comes down the luggage conveyor/ gets dumped in a pile outside the plane. Mark your bags to distinguish them from everyone else's standard black luggage. Duct tape around the handle always helps

Also, if you can cell-wrap it at the airport, might as well. The few extra dollars will be money well-spent when your bag comes back tamper-free, contents intact.

Bonus Advice: Exit the Plane at the Correct Destination

The flight left Ethiopia around 11:30 pm, and according to my schedule we were supposed to land in Rwanda at around 1:30 in the morning. After a few hours in the air, the plane starts to make its descent. I'm exhausted, and don't pay any attention to the pilot's announcement. As soon as the plane comes to a stop, I grab my bags, leave the plane, and walk to the arrivals terminal. I fill out a customs card, and then head to the visa line, as I don't have a visa for Rwanda. I hand over my passport; the immigration officer looks at it, looks at me, and asks why I'm in this line.

I need a visa.

You already have a visa.

No I don't.

At this point, he's getting a little exasperated, and flips through my passport to the Uganda visa.

Right, I say, but I'm in Rwanda.

And then it dawns on me. The plane was supposed to stop in Uganda en route to Rwanda.

I look at the customs card I just filled out, and

realize that it has Uganda spelled in large letters at the top.

At which point I grab my passport, grab my bags, and then run out of the arrivals hall, back onto the tarmac, and towards the airplane. No one stops me. At least until I get to the stairs leading up to the plane, at which point someone on the ground crew asks me—politely—what I'm doing. I'm supposed to be in Rwanda, I yell, wildly showing my boarding pass to everyone around me. No one seems to care, so I get back on the plane, much to the amusement of the flight attendants.

Lessons Learned:

1. Always listen to the fucking announcement.

2. People can be surprisingly reluctant to stop a crazy white person running through an airport. (M.B.)

Navigating the Airport

1. Arrive at the airport early enough to deal with unexpected delays. Bring your own snacks. A deck of cards never hurts.

2. If there's a line, wait patiently. If there's a scrum, be prepared to fight your way to the front. There are only the quick and the left-behind.

3. Travel with shoes that are easy to take on and off—not, say, knee-high boots.

4. Don't make eye contact with the customs' people. Just stare straight ahead and try not to look like you just swallowed a condom-full of Bolivian cocaine.

5. Split up your money, hiding it in various pouches and pockets.

6. The smaller the airline or airport, the more lax the security.

7. The poorer the country, the better the chance you'll be asked for a bribe at the airport.

8. Don't take pictures at the airport. Unless you want to be detained by various uniformed men looking for a bribe.

Flying, Or Knowing When Not To

Intracountry travel can be a harrowing experience, especially when the only flights available are UN-contracted death traps that seem to get cancelled as often as they actually depart. A few signs that you might want to wait for the next flight, or consider walking:

1. The plane smells like urine.

2. Your pilot appears to be hungover.

3. Your pilot is a drunk Ukranian named "Cuba."

4. They're trying to jumpstart the airplane with a car battery.

5. There's a mad scrum to board the airplane—no tickets, much less a line.

6. They're allowing livestock on board.

7. There don't appear to be any seatbelts.

8. They're allowing more passengers on board than there are seats.

9. You see duct tape. Anywhere.

10. The airline in question has crashed at least once in the past six months.

Bonus Advice: When to Let Bygones Be Bygones

Why do we trust pilots with our lives? One simple answer is that we really don't have a choice. You either trust the pilot, or you reconcile yourself to walking to Nairobi. But it goes deeper than that—fundamentally, we trust pilots because they wear uniforms. We assume that, at the very least, they don't pass out uniforms to just anyone. You have to have achieved some basic level of technical competence before they give you your epaulets.

Which made it all the more upsetting when the plane took off with its rear door hanging open. In the pilots' defense, we were in a small plane, and it was South Sudan. Still, one would think that even the most cursory pre-departure check would reveal that the back door was wide fucking open.

But no.

The first inkling we had that something was amiss came moments after takeoff, when the door began banging against the side of the plane. The three passengers turned around.

We stared at the open door.

We all turned back to stare at the pilots. At which point the co-pilot gave a "my bad" shrug, got up, gingerly walked to the rear of the plane—as said plane was flying a few hundred feet off the ground—reached out, and closed the door. (M.B.)

Negotiating with Cab Drivers

Let's make no mistakes. Cab drivers are not your friends. They will not treat you fairly. This is not a surprise. In most of the world, you might earn more in a week than they will over the entire year. Further, chances are you know relatively little about the city in which you find yourself, whereas the cab driver has been driving these streets/rutted roads/twisting alleyways for years.

You're probably also running late.

He—it's invariably a he—will charge too much. Far too much. You have two options:

(1) You can accept this with a zen-like state of calm. Counteroffer with half the fare. Settle on something like one-half to two-thirds of the original price. Consider the overpayment your small contribution to the local economy. Smile.

(2) You can get indignant. Let the cabbie know that you know that he's overcharging. Say that you live here, that you know how much the cab fare should cost. Raise your voice. Counteroffer with half the fare. Argue. Settle on something like one-half to two-thirds of the original price. Spend the balance of the ride fuming over the fact that you were ripped off.

Of course, none of this applies to your favorite cabbie—the one with whom you've developed a relationship, the one whose phone number is on speed dial in your phone, the one who drives you around on a regular basis. He's still overcharging you, but his services are, on the whole, worth more than gold. It is always important to find this favorite cabbie, and then be stingy about sharing his number with other expats. If you are too generous, within a matter of weeks he will be too busy to pick you up on time and you will be forced to find a new favorite.

How to Take a Shared Taxi

First off, try to get the front seat. You'll still share it with another passenger, but at least you'll be able to see where you're going. Barring that, aim for a seat by one of the backseat doors. Shoulder space comes at a premium when there are four people in the back of a 1980s sedan, and the best real estate is always on the edges. The same goes for minivans, with the exception of the no-man's land that constitutes the far back corner.

Since shared taxis almost always run on more-or-less fixed routes, it's crucial to know how these are determined and communicated. There's nothing worse than getting out of a taxi on the wrong side of town after 20 minutes of a squished, sweaty, death-defying race over bad roads. Sometimes final destinations are determined by the spot at which the taxi is parked. Other times, they're indicated by hand gestures shared between taxi drivers and potential passengers. If the latter, learn these well. You might think the difference between a finger pointed out versus down is subtle, but it can make all the difference.

If you're planning to take shared taxis often, we recommend a rigorous workout routine to improve both your lung capacity and general physical flexibility. Yoga classes are good places to start. Given the combination of human body odor and moldy car interior that inevitably permeates a shared taxi, you'll want to inhale the least possible number of times during the course of your journey. At the end of the day, all you can do is relax into it.

Driving Yourself: Basic Rules of the Road

Vehicle ownership marks an important milestone, from I-just-arrived to I'm-planning-on-staying-a-while. Besides, it's difficult to claim authenticity—much less any kind of expertise—if your entire stay in a given country is spent re-enacting a colonial version of *Driving Miss Daisy*.

Driving is also a wonderfully Darwinian way of building confidence, given the fact that traffic in most third-world cities consists of battered Toyota Corollas playing chicken with overloaded and/or brightly-painted diesel lorries. Not to mention a near-complete absence of stop signs and functioning traffic lights.

That said, traffic etiquette is really no different than any other kind of etiquette—it simply involves understanding and following those guidelines by which society tries to impose a certain minimum level of order. Though the details vary from country to country, certain basic rules are universal:

1. Any sort of shared taxi or minivan will act as aggressively as possible at all times.

2. Never allow traffic going a different direction to have the right of way. And its corollary— yield only when absolutely necessary.

3. Size matters—armored vehicles and large lorries almost always have the right of way.

4. It's not cutting someone off if you can get away with it.

5. Use of the horn is not so much cautionary as existential.

6. Lane markers should be treated as subtle jokes by long-dead city planners, like amusing hieroglyphics.

Where the Streets Have No Name

Driving on the Wrong Side of the Road

The bad news: we, as a species, haven't yet evolved to the point where we can all agree to drive on one side of the road or the other. (Or, for that matter, agree to use the same kind of electrical current.) Which means there's a decent chance you'll wind up driving in a country where they go the wrong way down the street. Since it's probably unrealistic to expect an entire nation to suddenly see the error of its ways and change its driving habits accordingly, it's you that will have to adapt.

The good news: it's not that hard to make the switch to local custom—you only have to make a left hand turn into oncoming traffic once, or at most twice, before the vision of your life flashing before your eyes shows you the error of your ways.

City Driving vs. Highway Driving

The difference between playing chicken at 15 and 75 miles per hour. (Or, for the metric minded, at 25 and 120 km per hour.)

Roundabouts

Any traffic system designed around the expectation that everyone can—and will—yield and merge simultaneously represents, at best, the triumph of hope over experience. Not to mention that, in any given third-world city, the number of cars has increased far beyond the original carrying capacity of the roads. This is bad enough when everyone is traveling in more or less a straight line. It becomes impossible when you force everyone to drive around in circles.

Think of, say, massively clogged arteries, and you get the idea.

Potholes

Everything tends towards entropy. Especially

poorly constructed, poorly maintained asphalt roads in countries that experience heavy rain. The miracle is that there are any roads left at all.

That said, there are two kinds of potholes—first are those that have been around so long they've become an accepted feature of the landscape. Eventually, you even begin to use them as landmarks when giving directions.

Then there are those potholes that emerge suddenly, seemingly overnight—vast geological disturbances large enough to snap an axel. There's no way to prepare, no amount of local knowledge that can save you. Which, granted, adds a certain level of excitement to what would otherwise be a relatively routine morning commute.

Use potholes to your advantage. For example, in heavily potholed areas, you can always tell the drunk drivers from the sober ones—they're the crazies driving in a straight line. Everyone else is swerving. Yes, it's counter to how you've come to identify drunk drivers in your hometown, but sometimes things get topsy-turvy in the midst of infrastructural deficits.

Finally, and needless to say, it's always best to try and avoid potholes. When that becomes impossible, however, your best bet is to take them either under 15 miles an hour or over 60, *Dukes of Hazzard* style. That said, anything deeper than 10 inches should be taken at less than 15 miles per hour.

High Beams

People will drive with their high beams at night. Which is understandable, given the lack of streetlights. Truly considerate drivers turn off their high beams when they see a car approaching the other way. Very few drivers are considerate. Plan accordingly.

Having said that, the use of flashing high beams and hazard lights can mean something in certain cities; learn what it is and then do it too.

Accidents

It sounds heartless, but if you get into a car accident—especially in a poorer area known for mob justice, and most especially if you injure someone—do not to get out of the car, unless you can get out and help without attracting a crowd. Instead, keep driving. Drive to the nearest police station and turn yourself in. And if you can call a medical facility en route, even better, particularly if there are functioning ambulances in-country.

The police station will, at best, involve massive amounts of paperwork, and more probably a large bribe and/or spending time in a jail cell under conditions you might not wish on your worst enemy. This is still preferable to being lynched, and, under most circumstances, involving the police is the best and fastest way to actually get help at the site of the collision. Safety first. For you and any bystanders.

Taking the Bus

Taking the bus is slow. It's uncomfortable. There won't be air conditioning. The number of people on a bus will always be approximately twice the number of actual seats. There's also a chance that you'll wind up at the bottom of a ravine.

On the other hand, taking the bus—especially

between cities—is incredibly cheap. The scenery can also be quite nice. The cost-benefit analysis is up to you.

Impressing Your Friends with Ethnic Curios

Half the joy of traveling is thinking about impressing people at home with your stories. Of course, once you're actually home, it's somewhat tacky to start every conversation with, "When I was in Myanmar..."

Ethnic curios are a wonderful way to let people know that you spent years overseas without having to mention that point explicitly. Pretentious, yes, but effective.

(Actually purchasing said curios is much like haggling over a taxi. You will get ripped off. Counteroffer for between a third and half the asking price, and settle for something slightly more.)

The challenge is choosing the right ethnic objects with which to decorate your one-bedroom apartment. Some tried and true guidelines:

1. Everyone buys masks. Don't buy a mask.

2. Don't buy—much less frame—any "native" art mass produced in China.

3. And the corollary: it's best if your curios were actually produced in your country of purchase. South African trinkets bought in West Africa just don't feel all that authentic, even if the giftee won't know the difference.

4. Similarly, nothing purchased at an airport will gain you any respect.

5. If that piece of art looks ugly in the market, it will look even uglier on your wall at home.

6. Rugs are nice.

7. Unique objects are even better. (Unique being defined as "something people at home probably haven't seen before.") Especially if there's actually a story you can tell about how you came to own said object.

Interacting with the Home Front

Living away from home can be hard, especially when traveling home and then back again entails many, if not all, of the hassles described above. Thus, it will be important to learn a few important communication strategies to stay in touch with friends and family from far away. The most basic include:

(1) Embrace technology, but do so with patience. Learn to love SIM cards, and switch between them strategically, depending on competing long distance calling rates. Teach your parents how to use Skype. It will be slow and intermittent, but this is to your advantage. It's a great excuse not to chat too long about all the things you're missing or having to describe all the things you're experiencing that they won't be able to understand.

(2) Develop an adaptable but consistent response to the question: "What do you do?" This should be appropriately self-mocking, and should preempt the assumption that you are, in some way or another, trying to "save the world." Best to knock down pedestals early and often, before you

are expected to actually somehow live up to that kind of nonsense.

(3) Get used to telling friends that you won't be able to make the wedding/reunion/birthday/baptism-of-their-first-child. Be strategic in which ones you DO attend, opting usually for maximum attendance of other friends, so you'll manage to kill as many birds as possible with one stone (i.e., expensive plane ticket).

Note: blogging or mass emailing should be carefully considered in advance of any attempts. We ourselves, of course, are guilty of using both, but the pros and cons should be dutifully weighed before jumping headlong into either. The same is true of how you use Facebook and Twitter. Remember: what goes on the internet, stays on the internet—for all to see, including local colleagues, partners, politicians, and future employers.

The Only Piece of Travel Advice that Really Matters

Shit will invariably go wrong. Relax. Do your best to develop a zen-like state of detachment.

2

HOW TO STAY HEALTHY

Your time overseas will, on a gastrointestinal level, consist of an extended game of Russian Roulette. Sometimes you win. Often you lose. You won't know which times are which until it's too late. That said, there are plenty of preventative measures you can take to limit your susceptibility. Good hygiene is one. Keeping your vaccinations up-to-date is another.

The key is to avoid as many avoidable illnesses as possible, and then to learn how to turn other, unavoidable illnesses to your advantage. Though diarrhea, vomiting, and a fever are not fun in and of themselves, they do provide excellent excuses for getting out of work and/or social engagements you'd rather miss. Learning to fake such symptoms is also useful.

Actually working while ill is also an excellent way to prove your dedication to the cause—whatever that cause might be—as long as you don't get all of your friends and colleagues ill in the process. Everyone admires a little martyrdom, but no one particularly wants to hang out with Typhoid Mary.

Finally, and needless to say, the information below comes from our own, personal experience, supplemented by useful (i.e., free) medical reference sites online. If you feel ill—or, worse, continue to feel ill—definitely see a doctor.

What to Pack in Your Med Kit

Men

In no particular order: Immodium, Cipro, Neosporin, antifungal cream, cortisone cream, eye drops, a few packets of Sudafed, Paracetamol (a.k.a., Tylenol, for the Americans among us), Nighttime Tylenol/Paracetamol, a few bandaids, condoms, antimalarial medication, a few packets of Theraflu, a few packets of Gatorade powder (in case you get dehydrated).

A bottle of water is also useful. As is toilet paper. Do not forget to pack some emergency toilet paper.

Women

See above. Add your "feminine hygiene product" of choice. Consider self-heating adhesive pads as well.

How to Use a Squat Toilet

There's no shame in placing your hands on the ground in order to steady yourself. Then again, this approach is somewhat dependent on the cleanliness of the squat toilet in question. At least be sure to balance forward, on your toes. The very last thing you want is to fall backwards. Practicing squats is also useful for balance, especially if the pit latrines in your area haven't been cleaned in a long time.

Dealing with Diarrhea When There's No Toilet Around

You knew that you shouldn't have eaten the fish. Or that hand-ground peanut butter. Or the grilled meat that was sitting in the sun for hours. But, well, bygones are bygones, and now you're traveling in the middle of nowhere, with nary a bathroom in sight.

You really have two options. First, take copious amounts of Immodium. Which won't necessarily solve the underlying problem, but—out of sight, out of mind. Particularly potent when combined with antibiotics like Cipro.

The second option is to let nature take its course.

This is unpleasant, especially if there are no strategically placed shrubs, bushes, trees, or hills around.

Say, in the desert.

If you're traveling with friends, you can always ask them to hold a towel or small sheet in front of you, to provide a little privacy. Which is also an excellent way of separating out your real friends from more fair-weather acquaintances.

It's even more unpleasant if you forgot to bring your own emergency toilet paper. Do not forget to bring your own emergency toilet paper.

Bonus Advice: What To Do When You Shit Yourself

The first time I shat myself was in the Dubai airport, of all places. I'd left Kabul the day before, and only had a single night in Dubai before flying on the next day to a new position in Nairobi. So, I decided to make the best of it, and throw caution to the wind. Which, in the circumstances, meant ordering the fish at a generic English pub in some forgettable Dubai neighborhood.

A decision I regretted almost immediately. After a night in my hotel room, merrily vomiting every hour on the hour, I thought the worst was over. I got to the airport in one piece, checked in, and made it through security. Then, in the midst of the duty-free emporium that is the Dubai airport, I farted. Except it wasn't a fart. Farts don't run down your leg.

So, I did what any self-respecting person would do. I panicked. It was only after a few moments hyperventilating, as people around me began to sniff the air, that I realized that more direct action was necessary. I cleaned myself off as well as I could in the nearest bathroom, and then gingerly—very gingerly—walked to a nearby clothing store, where I grabbed jeans and new underwear.

I did not take the nice salesperson up on her offer to "try it on and see if it fits." (M.B.)

Telling Good Shit from Bad Shit

The Bristol Stool Scale (no, really)—developed by Dr. Ken Heaton at the University of Bristol— classifies shit into seven different categories, as follows:

Type 1: Separate hard lumps, like nuts (hard to pass)

Type 2: Sausage-shaped but lumpy

Type 3: Like a sausage but with cracks on its

surface

Type 4: Like a sausage or snake, smooth and soft

Type 5: Soft blobs with clear cut edges (passed easily)

Type 6: Fluffy pieces with ragged edges, a mushy stool

Type 7: Watery, no solid pieces, entirely liquid

Generally speaking, types 1 and 2 indicate constipation, types 3 and 4 are considered normal, and types 5 through 7 indicate some level of diarrhea.

As for colors, just know that a bleeding ulcer can turn poop tarry black. Intestinal or anal bleeding can turn poop red, though this can also be the result of eating certain foods, like beets. Needless to say, bloody poop is never a good sign. Green poop can result from eating large amounts of leafy green vegetables; it can also be associated with diarrhea, when the body doesn't absorb as much iron.

Finally, if you know—or strongly suspect—

that more than half of your friends are suffering from diarrhea more than half the time, then you can safely assume that conversations about your digestive track (and the problems therein) will be met with polite curiosity, if not outright interest.

How to Deal with Malaria

First of all, don't get it. Seriously. It's really easy not to. There are a number of inexpensive prophylaxes available. If you happen to be like us, however, and wind up taking your pills sporadically, or not at all—usually out of some misguided bravado or perhaps concern about "long-term use"—then this advice might be too little too late.

The basic symptoms of malaria include some combination of fever, chills, headache, sweats, fatigue, and nausea and vomiting. Symptoms will often appear in cycles, and can appear anywhere from seven to forty days after the initial infection.

If you fear you do have malaria, then:

1. Get tested immediately.

2. Check and double-check the results—second

opinions are a good thing, especially if the first exam cost you 50 cents at the nearest one-room clinic. Malaria is one of the most "over-diagnosed" diseases out there, or so says one of our doctors.

3. Start taking meds immediately—better the wrong meds than a cerebral meltdown.

4. Whine; you're allowed.

5. Call home, it's worth the expense.

6. Rest—it's going to take less time than you'd imagine to feel mostly better, but longer than you think to feel fully better.

Bonus Advice: Take Your Malaria Prophylaxis

The first time I got malaria was, as is often the case, the worst. No, actually, that's not true: the fourth (and most recent) time I got malaria was the worst, but only because it was an unexpected relapse that struck while Christmas'ing in Athens. Talk about unfair.

But anyway, the first time was definitely the

scariest. I'd started getting sick on a Friday, and being new to West Africa, and thus not knowing how to get help or who to call, I decided to ride out the weekend in the hopes that my body aches and fever were "just" the flu and/or might miraculously go away on their own.

Besides, I told myself: people here live and work with malaria all the time. Right? Right. Surely if they can do it, so can I. Right?

Wrong.

By Monday my fingernails had turned blue and my bedroom walls had begun to undulate. By the time my coworkers showed up to rescue me, in response to my hysterical phone call, I could barely move, let alone walk. They all but dragged me down to the car, before starting a frantic round of phone calls to determine which hospital was our best bet. In a country that boasted only 50-60 local, legitimately-licensed doctors to serve a population of 3.5 million, this was not as simple a question as you might think.

We ultimately aimed our nose for the UN-base hospital, just on the outskirts of town.

Though technically not supposed to be admitted entrance, the guards took one look at our white car, with my white convulsing self in the back, and waved us through. The doctors were similarly sympathetic. Turns out, on top of the malaria, I had also contracted walking pneumonia, and the lack of oxygen accounted for my blue nails and hallucinations.

My hospital stay was tedious and lonely. For three days, every four hours, a Jordanian male nurse would come inject my IV with some medicine that, no joke, made my vagina burn for the first five seconds. Trying to tell him this, given the linguistic and cultural barriers, proved an exercise in futility. He only got embarrassed, and I can only imagine what he thought I was trying to say. Once, while taking myself down the hall to the bathroom, my 1950s-esque IV fell out of my arm, and I begun gushing thick red blood all over the hallway. Gross. It was still there the next day, albeit brown and dried. Even grosser.

I'd come without my glasses, without a book, without my laptop, and without my phone charger.

On the first night, once the phone died, I had nothing to do but stare at the out-of-focus ceiling. Fortunately, friends came the next day bearing clean underwear, portable electronics, and bootleg DVDs. These things only made the stay bearable; they did not make it pleasant.

I checked myself out a few days earlier than recommended, in order to catch a flight home that I'd had scheduled for months. As I left I promised that I would start taking my malaria prophylaxis. I meant it at the time. I really did. It just wasn't a promise I was ever able to keep, something my immune system will forever hate me for. (L.G.)

How to Deal with Parasites

Be prepared for the long haul. Parasites can be nasty buggers to detect, and even nastier to get rid of. Find a good doctor. And deworm at regular intervals, just to be safe. Make your deworming experience a group activity; it'll make it seem more like an adventure than a necessary precaution to avoid the possibility that you recently caught something microscopic that is slowly turning your intestines inside-out.

Eating and Drinking 101

There's a lot you can do to reduce the risk of a diarrhea disaster or other bacterial backlash, most of which just involves basic hygiene practices.

The following tips come from the US Centers for Disease Control and Prevention's (CDC) website (visit http://www.cdc.gov), and are usually only religiously practiced by the fly-in/fly-outers. Chances are, if you're really living in the place, the below will be, at best, unrealistic for 100% of the time and, at worst, outright absurd nearly 100% of the time. Nonetheless, we offer them here as a reminder of why it's probably your own fault that you got sick:

1. If you drink water, buy it bottled or bring it to a rolling boil for 1 minute before you drink it. Bottled carbonated water is safer than uncarbonated water.

2. Ask for drinks without ice unless the ice is

made from bottled or boiled water. Avoid popsicles and flavored ices that may have been made with contaminated water.

3. Eat foods that have been thoroughly cooked and that are still hot and steaming.

4. Avoid raw vegetables and fruits that cannot be peeled. Vegetables like lettuce are easily contaminated and are very hard to wash well.

5. When you eat raw fruit or vegetables that can be peeled, peel them yourself. (Wash your hands with soap first.) Do not eat the peelings.

6. Avoid foods and beverages from street vendors. It is difficult for food to be kept clean on the street, and many travelers get sick from food bought from street vendors.

Other Diseases You Might Wish to Avoid

The information below is also taken from the CDC website. Note how similar the symptoms are for most of the below. Trying to self-diagnose is likely an exercise in acute anxiety production. We definitely recommend seeing a real doctor if you're sick, provided, of course, there is one to be found.

Cholera

Cholera is acute diarrheal disease caused by—surprise, surprise—the bacteria vibrio cholerae. It's transmitted by contaminated food or water. The early stages of severe cholera (5-10% of all cases) are marked by: profuse watery diarrhea, vomiting, a rapid heart rate, thirst, muscle cramps, dry mucous membranes, and loss of skin elasticity (which—whatever that means—certainly doesn't sound good).

If untreated, severe cholera can cause severe dehydration, leading to renal failure, coma and death. According to the CDC, if you do find yourself caring for a cholera patient, it's an excellent idea to wash your hands as frequently as possible (and to dispose of any contaminated items).

Dengue

Dengue fever is transmitted by mosquitoes, who themselves become infected by biting a person who already has dengue. The disease cannot be spread directly from one person to another.

Symptoms include high fever, severe headache, pain behind the eyes, joint, muscle and bone pain, a rash, and mild bleeding from the nose or gums. The fever usually lasts two to seven days.

According to the CDC: "There is no specific medication for treatment of a dengue infection. Persons who think they have dengue should use analgesics (pain relievers) with acetaminophen and avoid those containing aspirin. They should also rest, drink plenty of fluids, and consult a physician. If they feel worse (e.g., develop vomiting and severe abdominal pain) in the first 24 hours after the fever declines, they should go immediately to the hospital for evaluation."

Ebola

Don't get ebola.

If you're in an area suffering from an ebola outbreak, it's probably best to leave. Immediately.

If you can't leave, then at the least, don't touch the blood or secretions of an infected person. Which, really, should go without saying.

Meningitis

Basic symptoms include a high fever, headache, and a stiff neck—other possible symptoms are nausea, vomiting, and discomfort looking into bright lights, confusion, and sleepiness. (Tragically, this often makes meningitis rather hard to distinguish from after-effects of drinking cheap gin.)

Bacterial meningitis can be treated with antibiotics, but treatment should be started as quickly as possible.

As the CDC helpfully notes: "Appropriate antibiotic treatment of most common types of bacterial meningitis should reduce the risk of dying from meningitis to below 15%, although the risk is higher among the elderly."

There's no treatment for viral meningitis, but

most people recover on their own. Antibiotics won't help cure viral meningitis. As with all diseases in this section, seek medical help immediately if you think you might have meningitis.

Rabies

Rabies is often transmitted through the bite of an infected animal, most often dogs. If you have been bitten, immediately wash the wound with soap and water for five to ten minutes (also use an antiseptic iodine if available) and then contact a doctor. Post-exposure prophylaxis is effective in treating the disease, but only if administered quickly.

The CDC recommends that patients receive a dose of human rabies immunoglobulin, as well as four doses of rabies vaccine (the first dose immediately after exposure, and then on the third, seventh, and fourteenth days after the initial dose). If you've already received the pre-exposure vaccine, then you do not need the immunoglobulin, and only the first two doses of vaccine.

And, really, if you are bitten, get checked immediately. According to the CDC: "It's important to remember that rabies is a medical urgency but not an emergency. Decisions should not be delayed." Which, translated into common-speak, means "don't be a idiot." Because, if left untreated, rabies is almost invariably fatal.

At the least, please ignore that urge to pet stray animals, especially if said animals are acting strangely and/or frothing at the mouth.

Tuberculosis

Tuberculosis—TB to its friends—is spread through the air "when a person with active TB disease of the lungs or throat coughs, sneezes, speaks, or sings." It's unclear why the CDC felt the need to add singing to the list of dangerous activities, but forewarned is forearmed.

The CDC also helpfully notes that TB is not (repeat not) spread by: shaking hands, sharing food or drink, touching bed sheets or toilet seats, sharing toothbrushes, or kissing.

It is, at this point, worth pausing for a moment and trying to imagine just how bizarre it must be working at the CDC, where singing is classified as a potentially hazardous activity, but where the touching of toilet seats is perfectly acceptable. (Also, how do you share bed sheets—much less a toothbrush—with someone and not talk to them? Methinks folks at the CDC probably don't date much.)

To make matters somewhat more complicated, "not everyone infected with TB bacteria becomes sick." A person with a latent TB infection has no symptoms, doesn't feel sick, and can't spread TB. That said, treatment is still necessary to prevent a latent infection from becoming active. (Latent TB infections can usually be detected through skin or blood tests.)

The symptoms for active TB include a bad cough lasting three weeks or longer, chest pain, coughing up blood or sputum, weakness or fatigue, weight loss, loss of appetite, chills, fever and night sweats. Or as the CDC summarizes, a person with active TB "usually feels sick."

If you have active TB, seek treatment, not least because you're at risk of spreading it to others. TB can be treated by taking a course of drugs for six to twelve months. Failure to follow the regimen means you could become sick again, as well as contribute to the creation of drug resistant strains of the disease.

Typhoid

You can get typhoid by eating or drinking items handled by someone with typhoid, or if sewage contaminates the water you use to drink or wash food. As the Centers for Disease Control and Prevention helpfully note: "Therefore, typhoid fever is more common in areas of the world where handwashing is less frequent and water is likely to be contaminated with sewage." The CDC also recommends two straightforward ways to avoid getting typhoid: avoid risky foods and drinks (e.g., frozen ice concoctions sold by the side of the road) and—seeing as it's not always possible to avoid "risky" foods—get vaccinated.

Symptoms include a sustained high fever (103° to 104° F), stomach pains, headache and/or loss of appetite. Some people also develop a rash. If you think you might have typhoid, see a doctor and get a stool or blood test immediately. Typhoid is usually treated using antibiotics. Without treatment, the fever can last for weeks or months, and can at times be fatal.

Yellow Fever

We threw this in here just for kicks. Yellow fever vaccines are pretty much mandatory for most expat travel, and you will learn to carry your yellow fever vaccine card with a certain amount of pride—it is, after all, your entry ticket to the expat club.

How to Act Like a Martyr

Everyone works sick—you'll get no sympathy for low-grade fevers. That said, you will get sympathy if people think that you're working through a serious illness. (As long as such illness is not contagious.)

It's best to claim symptoms that are either easily faked, or hard to disprove. For instance, don't claim you have malaria unless you can sweat on cue, and also raise your core body temperature at will. Fortunately, vicious hangovers have many of the same symptoms as more serious maladies. Unfortunately, most of your coworkers were probably witnesses to your debauchery the night before. This is not a problem if you do most of your drinking alone.

Claiming acute gastronomic distress is always an option, as long as you're willing to spend hours each day on the toilet. If so, make sure to keep a book or magazine close to hand, to deal with the inevitable boredom. Moaning softly also helps.

Most importantly, don't overdo it. The key to martyrdom is to do just enough to convince everyone that you're on death's door, but to never utter a word of complaint. Needless to say, this is much easier to achieve when faking an illness than suffering from one.

3.

FOOD AND DRINK

Old fish. Sorghum with green, mucus-like sauce. Gristly goat swimming in oil. The search for culinary authenticity ends, more often than not, with the realization that pre-packaged, mass produced food isn't so bad after all. As Chris Rock said, it's not red meat that kills you; it's green meat.

As a corollary: local, more authentic food (defined as what everyone else is eating) isn't necessarily better, much less more healthy, especially if everyone else tends to be either incredibly poor, or farmers who depend on heavy meals to sustain them during a day in the fields. Also don't look for healthy local food in cultures that prize men with large bellies and/or rubenesque women.

As a quick rule of thumb: if you're in an area

where different cultures have been interacting, fighting, fucking, and generally sloshing around for centuries, chances are the food is relatively decent. Which generally means the coasts. The further inland you go, the greater the chance that the local culture has spent centuries perfecting various ways to eat sorghum.

How to Eat with Your Hands

Eat with the right. Do not, under any circumstances, eat with the left. The left is for other things. Bathroom things.

How to Pretend You Like Local Food

Sometimes common courtesy requires that you eat foods you would otherwise prefer to avoid. The key things to remember:

1. If you're hungry enough, you'll eat anything.

2. Assuming that you're eating by choice as opposed to necessity, the key is to consume as little as possible while being as polite as

possible. The same rules apply as when you were eight—eat slowly, take small bites, and keep moving the food around your plate.

3. Cheap gin or whiskey is an excellent way to cut the taste, and also erase all memories of the experience.

4. If neither cheap gin nor whiskey is available, a Coke chaser will do in a pinch. Pepsi, Sprite, or other soft drinks also work, but they are never as readily accessible as Coke, whose billboards you will see in every country you'll ever visit.

5. Hot sauce—added liberally—makes almost anything more palatable. Or at least obscures any unpleasant (albeit authentic) tastes and flavors.

6. You will get sick drinking local water. You will never get sick drinking bottled water, soda, or beer. That said, it's up to you to judge the short-term benefits and long term costs of subsisting on soda and beer. (That expat fifteen-pound gain being, on the whole, quite similar to the

fifteen pounds you gained your freshman year
of college.)

7. Biscuits in their original package might taste
like a mixture of chemicals and sawdust, but
they'll never make you sick.

8. Only eat fish if there's actually an ocean, sea,
river, or lake somewhere nearby.

9. Amateurs, after a few bites, plead a
stomachache or other digestive distress.
Seasoned veterans, after a few bites, smile
bravely and plead a pre-existing stomachache,
thereby excusing the need to eat more while
also gaining valuable martyr points. Real
professionals remark casually upon their
preexisting stomach conditions in advance of
the meal, just in case. All in all, this creates a
win-win situation. Either (a) you will consume
an entire dish despite your ailment, which will
gratify your hosts; or (b) you can refuse most of
your meal without causing offense, given your
gastrointestinal distress.

Choosing a Restaurant

For all the ills of colonialism, it did have some benefits. Namely the fact that you can get decent pastries across most of francophone Africa. In fact, centuries of globalization have produced something of a common culinary pidgin, a true international cuisine built mostly on French fries and the spread of Chinese and Indian restaurants to every corner of the globe. Not to mention the floating world of expatriate restaurants that follow aid workers and journalists from disaster to disaster and conflict to conflict. Which is how you find Thai food in both Kabul and Monrovia.

Yet the question still remains—how to choose a restaurant in a country or city you barely know?

1. Are other foreigners eating there? If yes, it's probably not "authentic" *per se*, but there's also a relatively low chance that you'll get sick. If you're the only foreigner in the place, it's probably quite authentic, though chances are better than even that you'll spend the evening hunched over a toilet. At least the first few

times you go.

2. That said, it's hard to go wrong—or get sick—from food grilled right in front of you. Otherwise, gravitate towards restaurants where you can't see the kitchen, ignorance being bliss.

3. If you do go the Chinese or Indian route, try to choose a Chinese or Indian restaurant that's staffed by the nationality in question.

4. Clean utensils are usually a decent indication of the cleanliness of the restaurant as a whole. Or, more accurately, dirty utensils are always a bad sign.

5. Flies are alright. Rats are not alright. At least visible rats.

6. You will be disappointed by the pizza outside of the US and, possibly, Italy. You will also be disappointed in the hamburgers.

7. Street food looks delicious. There's also a decent chance it will give you typhoid. Especially if it involves flavored ice.

What Not to Drink

Human ingenuity being what it is, there's always something to drink. Even in countries where alcohol is illegal. In some ways, being able to procure and consume bootleg alcohol in a place like Darfur is nothing less than the triumph of the human spirit over incredible odds.

Of course, it tastes horrible. And, it could leave you blind. There are, roughly speaking, two kinds of horrible alcohol. The first is simply cheap alcohol manufactured in a place you wouldn't expect. Like, say, Asmara Dry Gin. It probably won't kill you, or maim you, but it will leave you with a vicious hangover. On the plus side, it can also be used to strip varnish.

The second is bootleg alcohol—most often available in places where (a) producing, purchasing, or consuming alcohol is technically illegal, or (b) where a significant percentage of the population is too poor to buy alcohol in stores.

Here things get a little dicey. On the one hand, drinking bootleg alcohol makes you feel wonderfully hardcore. It's also an excellent way to get very drunk very quickly. On the other, it might kill you. Especially if it's cut with formaldehyde or methanol. As always, proceed with caution.

How to Make Horrible Alcohol Drinkable

The same rules apply overseas as applied in college—copious amounts of Coca-Cola, Pepsi, or fruit juice (think tropical medley) will make almost any cheap alcohol palatable. Or palatable enough.

Bonus Advice: Purchasing Alcohol in Sudan

I've never wanted a drink as badly as I did in countries that banned alcohol. Yet another example of how nothing tips the scales between functional and complete alcoholism quite like prohibition. Which is how I found myself standing outside the Amarat semi-supermarket on a busy Khartoum street one night, waiting for a Copt to arrive with two bottles of black market Asmara Dry Gin.

After about fifteen minutes an old Corolla

pulled up, and a man with an impressive perm sidles over, asking if I'm "Michael." I nod and smile, at which point he hustled me into the car as quickly as possible. I gave him directions to my apartment, and we completed the purchase on the poorly lit and mostly empty street near the house. As I got out of the car, the bottles banged against the door. He winced and sped away.

It occurred to me later that gangly Americans don't really blend into the background in Sudan, and that perhaps I shouldn't have arranged our meeting in a conspicuously public place.

Similarly, it might have also been a good idea to come up with a pseudonym while negotiating an illegal alcohol purchase over my mobile phone.

That said, all's well that ends well, and the Asmara Dry Gin helped ensure that evening's party was as festive as possible. It's a fine drink, as long as there's plenty of cola or juice to mask the turpentine flavor. We also had cheap Bulgarian vodka, which goes quite well with a homemade fruit punch. (M.B.)

4

LEARNING TO LOVE THE EXPAT BUBBLE: FASHION, FRIENDS, AND FUCKING

There are two unmistakable signs that you live in an expat bubble. First, the only time that you talk to non-expats is at work, or while shopping in the market, or while talking to your housekeeper or cook.

Second, you look around at any social gathering and realize that no one—no one—is actually from the country where said gathering is actually taking place.

As always, you have choices. You can strike out proudly on your own, boast of your friendships with local shopkeepers and street children, and tell everyone and anyone that you didn't travel overseas to spend your time drinking with Americans and Europeans.

This is an honorable path. It will also, more likely than not, leave you very lonely. Especially if you ever have any desire to talk about something other than work or politics.

Alternatively, you can embrace the expat bubble. Like any social situation in which a group of random people is confined to a relatively small space—say high school, or prison—the expat bubble promises immediate (albeit transitory) friendship, neverending drama, and the wonderful opportunity to scorn the newly-arrived.

It's easy to moralize, and say that it's wrong to live in a bubble, that you cut yourself off from understanding—or even trying to understand—the country in which you're living.

That said, it's also easier.

And sometimes, after a long, trying day or week or month, all you want to do is drink heavily with people who speak your native tongue. This is normal.

As ever, striking the right balance between these two extremes is up to you.

What to Wear

Expat fashion is something of an oxymoron. The great Sergio Valente once explained: "How you look tells the world how you feel." By this standard, most expats feel like crap. Men in rumpled chinos and short-sleeved shirts; women in faded jeans and long, tunic-like blouses. It's not just that everyone seems to wear the same thing, but that the uniform is so uniformly boring.

That said, there's a method to the madness. Expat fashion must steer a perilous course between two equally rocky shoals. On one side lies the ridicule that comes from trying to dress native. The only thing more ludicrous than a Western man in a shalwar kameez is a Western man trying to justify why he's wearing a shalwar kameez in the first place. On the other side lies the embarrassment that comes from dressing like a CNN correspondent, resplendent in a newly purchased action vest of many pockets.

The first choice screams that you're trying too hard, while the second loudly proclaims that your only previous experience of a foreign country was a weekend spent in Canada. As in any social milieu, expat fashion is, at the end of the day, all about showing that you belong.

Male Style: The Joys of Expat Chic

Most male expats dress alike—some variation on beaten-in chinos or jeans and a short sleeve button-down shirt. This approach has numerous benefits, not least of which is safety in numbers. You might not stand out, but nor will you risk becoming the laughingstock of Goma or Khartoum.

Consider wearing colors that don't show stains. Brown is good. Similarly, your clothing should also be able to withstand being washed with a detergent that has the consistency of gravel.

Needless to say, expensive clothes are probably a mistake. Other clothing to avoid: board shorts, wife-beaters, tight pants, any clothing with ironic messages, or anything you would wear for a night out in Williamsburg or Camden.

To Shave or Not to Shave

There are numerous advantages to not shaving. First, it makes you look older, which can be useful when you're living in a society that equates age with wisdom and responsibility. Especially if you're still in your twenties.

Second, a beard makes you look more hardcore, as though you've just spent the past few months deep, deep in the bush, far from any effeminate accoutrements like soap, much less running water.

This is particularly useful if you actually work at a desk all day, but wish to appear as though you don't. Don't go too far with the facial hair, however. Hair growth can reach a point of diminishing returns, and overly scraggly scruff starts to make you look crazy, as opposed to more badass.

Against all that, there's really only one reason to shave. In a world where everyone has a beard, or at least two weeks worth of scruff, going without shows some spark of individuality. Sort of like being a Republican in San Francisco.

Female Style: No, I'm Not a Whore

As a rule of thumb, it's best to err on the conservative side of the spectrum when it comes to picking out your outfit. No, of course, as strong, educated, motivated women we don't need to perpetuate unfair societal norms and expectations about the Piety of Woman, but fourth wave feminism is all about choices. So choose wisely in the wardrobe, sisters. Also, remember that there's no clear separation between work and play in the expat world, so how you dress for the latter will inevitably have some consequences for how people view you in the former.

If you're in a country where women cover up, do so also. Burqas are unnecessary, but invest in a lot of lightweight headscarves that can double as shawls or picnic blankets in other contexts. Elsewhere, especially hot climates, easily mix-and-matched skirts can get you far. Beware, however: mini-skirts might get you further than you'd intended. Pants are fine too; they can just get hot. It's really a matter of personal taste.

That said, defer often to local preference when it comes to style. Pay particular attention to the clothing for which you receive compliments. If said compliments come from a woman, rewear the outfit often. If they come from a man, perhaps consider adjusting the neckline up and the hemline down.

As with men, sturdy fabrics and/or inexpensive (and thus easily replaceable) materials are usually best. Delicates are, by their nature, delicate and unlikely to last that long under indelicate conditions. Irony and fashion statements don't translate well about 99% of the time. You can be "individual" in your choice of jewelry, if you must, but efforts to stand out on the fashion front rarely carry with them as much glamour or success as they might in Paris or Prague.

Bonus Advice: Dressing for a Date with Angelina Jolie

It took me over an hour to figure out what to wear. Which is somewhat embarrassing at the best of times, but all the more ludicrous given that I had exactly four shirts and three pairs of pants. It's one thing to be defeated by your wardrobe—it's quite another when your wardrobe contains a total of twelve possible combinations.

Then again, it's not every evening that you get to meet Angelina Jolie. A friend of mine—a man who worked in security, a man who knew things—had inadvertently let slip a few weeks before that Ms. Jolie was coming to Kabul, ostensibly to visit a UN project she supported.

I reacted with all the dignity one would expect. I begged. I pleaded. Anything for an invitation to the dinner that she was hosting at a local Italian restaurant. When he finally agreed to see what he could do, I cried tears of gratitude.

And now the big night was here. This was my one chance, but how to set myself apart, how to impress a gorgeous Hollywood actress? I cycled through those twelve possible sartorial combinations again and again, searching for the look that would say: "I've been in the shit, I've seen things, but I'm still a sensitive, slightly troubled man who needs the attentions of a famous actress to make whole."

Or something along those lines.

I finally settled on my second cleanest pair of jeans (beaten up, but not too beaten up), my cleanest long sleeve button-down shirt (to show that I was making an effort) and underneath—the coup de grace—a torn undershirt (to show that I wasn't one of those pansies who just sits in an office all day—I'd seen things, and had my shirt ripped in the process.)

A friend and I arrived at the restaurant at the appointed hour, mentioned the special password ("angel") to the Afghan man guarding the door, and were ushered to a back room. On the verge, just before he opened the door—on the edge of paradise—we high-fived.

And then the door swung open to reveal my security friend, surrounded by all our mutual friends, laughing and laughing as cameras flashed to record our shock and bewilderment. A semi-elaborate hoax. Made all the better when I noticed Angelina was missing, and asked if she'd gone to the bathroom. (M.B.)

How to Make Friends with Expats

The standard rules apply—be nice, be interested in what people say, don't twitch.

A little humility also goes a long way. There's really nothing more annoying than listening to someone who just arrived in a country expound on the complex sociopolitical-religious factors at play. Telling stories about how you almost died in airplane crashes in other poor, war-torn countries is a far better—and less pretentious—way to prove your bona fides.

And, most important, buy people drinks. Smoking, and bumming out cigarettes generously, is also a good way to bond.

Which Expats to Avoid

1. Anyone who twitches.

2. Anyone who can't make or maintain eye contact.

3. Anyone who drinks heavily during the day.

4. Anyone you slept with in another country,

especially if the words pregnancy or STD are likely to arise in conversation.

5. Anyone whose idea of a relationship is to carry on screaming, drunken fights in a public place.

6. Anyone who seems a little rapey.

7. Anyone who feels the need to explain to you— in excruciating detail, without being asked, and while sober—why you should consider him or her an expert on a given country or topic.

8. Anyone wearing sunglasses and/or a sidearm indoors. Unless, of course, you enjoy hanging around with private military contractors. In which case, see rapey, above.

9. Anyone who takes pride in not bathing.

Learning to Love the Expat Bar Scene

There's a small cottage industry of journalists who will fly into a not-so-nice place, and then do a story on how the international community likes to spend its evenings smoking, drinking, and sleeping around.

Depending on the circumstances, and the journalist's predilections, this story will have one of three slants—"dancing on the edge of the abyss," if the journalist is feeling introspective, "fucking in the face of death," if the journalist just got laid, or "look how these spoiled aid workers live compared to the misery all around" if the journalist is feeling like (a) scoring cheap points, and (b) didn't get laid.

These stories—especially the latter—tend to elicit the same reaction from those profiled: indignation mixed with charges of poorly researched sensationalism. And they are sensationalistic.

They're also more true than not.

People like to drink. Even more when they're stressed, need a distraction, and have absolutely nothing else to do in the evenings.

So, most large cities in less comfortable places will have an expat bar or two or three. It will be crowded. (Unless there's been a recent bomb scare, or suicide attack, or police crackdown.) It will be loud. You will pay far too much for mediocre drinks.

If you're female, you will enjoy a great deal of attention. If you're male, you will receive a great deal of attention from prostitutes, at least in Africa and Asia. (Though not so much in the Middle East.)

The expat bar is a wonderful place to get very, very drunk. It's also a wonderful place for more anthropological pursuits, where—if the conditions are right—one can see almost every species of war-zone and disaster porn expat gathered together in one place:

- Twenty-something aid workers drinking loudly in large groups.

- Thirty-something aid workers—looking somewhat worse for the wear—drinking in smaller groups.

- Journalists huddled together.

- Private sector or government contractors in suits and semi-sensible shoes.

- Private military contractors in short sleeve shirts and cargo pants, sometimes wearing sunglasses indoors.

- And, of course, older white men of indeter-
  minate background dancing with much, much
  younger local women.

At its best, it's like the cantina scene in Star
Wars. At its worse, it makes you embarrassed and
ashamed to be an expat. Of course, the two are
often the same.

How to Behave at a House Party

Make sure to bring your own booze. Get drunk.
Ignore people you don't know.

Bonus Advice: Having a Marching Band at Your Party

I knew it was a surprise party, I just didn't know
what the surprise was. In my limited experience,
surprise parties usually involved surprising the
guest of honor with the party itself, but that was
not the case in this instance. It was a friend's
farewell party, and he knew full well that it was

going on. He'd organized the guest list, and the booze trip, and the snacks. What he didn't know, however, was that his best friend had organized something else, too.

The Big Surprise showed up at midnight, resplendent with their brass and their percussion. Playing "When the Saints Go Marching In," the marching band came marching in themselves, right up the stairwell and into the living room-cum-dance floor. And then, after a few songs, they went marching out again, this time followed by a lot of drunken party goers. I'd like to say I was with them, but I wasn't. I watched from the balcony, thinking not only was this probably not all that safe, but also that it was probably pretty rude.

The poor neighbors probably had to get up in the morning, and here we were, a bunch of (mostly white) kids, lost in our own revelry. It was good music though. And a party to remember. (L.G.)

Romance in the Far Abroad

We all know people cheat. Expats are not alone in this. But imagine what happens to that old adage about out of sight out of mind when you're actually on different continents—especially when you happen to live in the sort of country where people tend not to bring their spouses, much less their children. This is where Facebook comes in handy.

If ever you develop a crush on another expat while abroad, the first step in pursuing a relationship is to make use of your social networking tools to determine if, in fact, he or she is already networked to someone else. (Which at this point, is probably something you already do, but thought we'd add it nonetheless.) Pursue this person if you wish. But know what you're getting into—99.9% of the time the person in question is not going to leave his or her partner for a tropical fling in some place too lonely for Lonely Planet. Unless, of course, that person is there precisely to get away from his or her partner. In which case the situation is probably messy and best not to get too emotionally attached.

If you do wind up meeting the man/woman of your dreams and they do happen to be single and, better yet, they like you back, take your time easing into it. While we know of a few romantic expat fairy tales, keep this in mind: Unless you're both interested in settling down or moving to the same country (even if one of you doesn't have a job or is willing to give up a job for what's best for the relationship), or are alright with long stretches of long distance—the longterm chances of success are slim, and it probably won't work.

The truth hurts, we know. That doesn't make it not the truth.

To Shag or Not to Shag

Far be it from us to suggest that abstinence is either realistic or desirable. That said, if you do decide to act on your carnal instincts, a few things to keep in mind:

1. Use protection. Seriously. Unless you enjoy spending weeks at a time worrying that you've

contracted an STD.

2. Try not to sleep with anyone at work. Failing that, try not to sleep with anyone whom you report to, or who reports directly to you.

3. Keep in mind that it will probably end awkwardly, especially as you both will (a) know all the same people, and (b) continue to see each other at parties—if not at work—for the foreseeable future.

4. On a related note—anything bad you say about someone will come back around, especially considering that you'll probably run into that same person again in a different country.

Bonus Advice: When Your Ex-Lover Sleeps With Your Friend

I remember it being a conscious decision: to get angry or not to care. I choose not to care because the truth is that I didn't. As I watched them kissing on the balcony—one of my best friends and one of my ex-lovers—all I could actually feel was bemusement about the situation. Was this really what my life had come to? It was the first time I thought that maybe, just maybe, I had been in the field for too long.

We'd met, he and I, at one of the only night clubs in town several months prior. I had been out on the prowl, mad at a different quasi-lover for not being loverly enough and on the lookout for someone who would be. We wound up elbow-to-elbow at the bar:

Me: "Buy a girl a drink?"

Him: "How about a whiskey?"

Me: "Shall we make it a shot?"

Him: "If you insist."

Two shots and some banal flirtation later:

Him: "I have more whiskey back at my flat, you know."

Me: "Do you, now?"

Him: "Hmmmm. I do indeed. Shall we go try it?"

Me: "If you insist."

For the next few weeks, while he was in town for his consultancy, we fell into a pretty comfortable rhythm. He'd come over to mine bearing booze and cigarettes. I'd make dinner. We'd eat dinner while drinking the booze and smoking the cigarettes. When everything was finished, most especially the booze, we'd go to bed. Sometime thereafter we'd go sleep. And then he left, and we didn't stay in touch. He was married, after all, and that had never been part of the plan.

And then a few months later he came back, as I'd known he would, and we tried on our rhythm again for size one more time. It had been fun, but it hadn't quite "fit" the way it used to, and we both tacitly agreed, without ever talking about it, to leave it there, as friends.

It was only a week later that I stumbled upon him and my friend making out on another friend's balcony. It was a Sunday evening, and we'd spent the day with a few other people saying farewell to our host in true expat fashion: with a whole lot of alcohol. And now here we were, several hours later, pissed out of our minds and prone to sloppy behavior.

I forgave them for it. And I gave them permission to go home together, claiming not to have a claim on him, and then I watched them walk up the hill to her house, and I honestly didn't care. That, more than anything, is what horrified me. Not his hedonism, not her disloyalty. My complete and utter uncaring. It wasn't who I wanted to be, and that's when I knew that maybe it was time to go home. (L.G.)

How to Handle an Affair

Simple—have no expectations that it's anything more than what it is. It's not.

How to Deal with Sexual Harassment

First things first: there's no such thing as a tattle-tale or a loud-mouth when it comes to sexual harassment. At least, not in the negative sense. In fact, if that casual flirtation is crossing the line, or if that guy on the street is becoming too aggressive, your best strategy is almost always to get more vocal. The last thing sexual harassers expect is confrontation, which is exactly why it's the best approach. Don't get shy; get angry. Turn around and tell him off. Look him in the eye and demand an apology. And if it just so happens that you've been the victim of a bicycle-by groping, spin around and hurl obscenities at his back. This is good, and not just because it will make you feel better (and it will). It will also draw a crowd, in which you'll find safety and support, and in which he (most sexual harassers are a "he," but of course there are exceptions) will find shame and embarrassment.

If the harassment is not just opportunistic, however, and is coming from someone with whom you work, it's a slightly different story. The same rule of thumb applies, though: don't stay silent. Let someone know the way they're acting makes you feel uncomfortable. Pull the "culture clash" card if you need to, and chalk it up to your prude Western upbringing. But if that doesn't work, and if you really feel uncomfortable, it's best to consult a real advice book, or, better yet, your happy (or, as is more often the case, your "not-so-happy") Human Resources person.

5

LEARNING THE EXPAT LINGO:
HOW TO TALK THE TALK

If you do find yourself working, living, drinking or sleeping with an aid worker or a journalist, it's still possible to fit in, and even contribute to the inevitable—and neverending—discussions about his or her work. A few simple rules to keep in mind:

1. Nod frequently. Look thoughtful. Especially when people are talking about either (a) horrific things, (b) how fucked up everything is, or (c) how awful their boss is.

2. Refer to Addis Ababa as Addis. Similarly, Johannesburg should always be Joburg.

3. Say ciao, even though you're not Italian.

4. Aid workers are notorious for speaking in acronyms. You might, after enough time

hanging out with aid workers, feel the irresistible urge to make up acronyms. This is healthy. Just remember that most acronyms are three or four letters long. Try to use the most common vowels and consonants. If you can't think of a decent three or four letter acronym on your own, then just use airport short codes—KHT, NBO, etc.

5. Acronyms describe processes or concepts that invariably sound or work better on paper than in practice. Hence, when using your new acronym—the NBO process—try to look thoughtful and frustrated and resigned, yet still willing to fight the good fight. In short, try to look just a little like a martyr. Also use the same expression when saying words like "governance," "participatory," or "sustainable." Use these words as frequently as possible.

How to Speak British English

As George Bernard Shaw once remarked, "England and America are two countries separated by the same language." Given the number of our Commonwealth cousins living in Africa and Asia and the Middle East, as well as the propensity of various Europeans to speak a bastardized form of British English, it's useful to learn how American English translates into British:

Awesome = brilliant. For instance: "They're fixing the potholes on the main drag?! Brilliant!"

To have sex with/screw/fuck = to shag. For instance: "Oh those two? Yeah, they're totally shagging, but he's married so they're trying to keep it secret."

College = university. For instance: "When I was at university I partied a lot, but I don't remember drinking quite as much as I used to when I worked in Sierra Leone."

Vacation = holiday. For instance: "Dear Boss, if I don't go on holiday soon, it's entirely possible that I will have a psychotic break. Please approve this holiday request."

Drunk = Smashed. For instance: "I was so smashed last night that I forgot I'd slept with her before."

And, last but not least, the annoying habit of abbreviating names and places when it's really not necessary. For instance, calling Baghdad "Baggers."

Cocktail Talk: Winning the Overseas Experience Game

1. Never brag openly about your experience. It's uncouth.

2. Similarly, never start a conversation by saying how long you've been in the country. This not only makes you seem insecure, but also leaves you open to embarrassment if your interlocutor has, in fact, been there longer than you have.

3. Even if the person has actually been in the country longer than you have, all is not lost. Ask where they were before, and then casually mention either that (a) you were there, but at a worse time, or (b) you spent the past few years in a country that was even more dangerous.

4. Finally, and most important, stockpile near

death experiences, especially involving third-world airlines. Instead of listing the number of countries where you've lived and worked, it's far more effective—not to mention socially acceptable—to prove your credentials by casually describing the time you almost crashed on a runway in the DRC or in the mountains over Kabul.

Proving You're an Expert in Three Easy Steps

A few months in a country doesn't make you an expert on the local politics or culture. Which, granted, has never stopped anyone from acting like a mere visit—no matter how short—confers some immediate knowledge about the country in question. The problem isn't so much the arrogance inherent in believing that you can comprehend—much less analyze—another society after a few days or weeks or months. The problem is trying to do so and failing miserably. Arrogance is bad, but sounding like an idiot is far worse.

Yet whereas real expertise is a rare commodity, sounding like an expert isn't all that difficult.

To that end, three simple rules for pontificating on the poverty stricken, war-torn country of your choice:

1. Memorize the names of various ethnic groups and semi-obscure towns. Ask questions like: "But what do the [insert name of random ethnic group] think?" Or "What about the situation in [semi-obscure town]?"

   Both of which are best said with a thoughtful expression, verging on concerned. There's nothing like seeming to agree with your interlocutor while subtly pointing out that his or her analysis is rather facile for ignoring the opinion of the Loma in Voinjama.

2. Memorize the date of one significant or semi-significant event in the country's history. Tie all current political and/or military developments back to that date: "You make an interesting point about Congolese politics, but it's all really just an outgrowth of what happened in 1965."

Don't deign to explain further; instead, act as though of course everyone should know what happened in Congo in 1965.

3. Listen to any explanation intently, think about it for a moment, then say: "Of course, it's never that simple," or "It's always more complicated." Don't feel the need to offer any additional information.

How to Talk to Journalists

If you are a Westerner living in a non-tourist-trafficked place—especially if something horrible is currently happening, or happened in the very recent past—there's a decent chance you'll meet journalists.

There's also a decent chance that these journalists—working on deadline, and desperate for a quote—will ask your views on the situation. To that end, it's useful to have a sense of what journalists actually want when they approach you, looking harried and somewhat disheveled. We took a quick, completely unscientific poll of various journalists to get a sense of what kind of information they want—and don't want—when they speak to aid workers and other expats.

According to one reporter:

> Key thing for me is dynamics of the situation: what's driving the conflict, who are the players, what are their motivations, what are the economic factors, where does money come in, how does it go forward? In a way, what we don't want is even more important: i.e., we all need to resist the temptation to recycle ever-increasing numbers of victims, often based on nothing more than guesstimates that the echo-chamber of NGOs-media turns into gospel. Always in the market for people willing to put crisis in perspective rather than hype!

Other journalists provided the following thoughts on what they want when trying to report on a story:

- "Transport, especially assisted passage into parts of world otherwise difficult to access."

- "Help with fixers, hotels, etc." (This is usually directed by the agency PR person, as is above.)

- "Someone who can speak the language of his or her audience." (Especially if it's TV or radio.)

- "Humanitarian stories that are either disasters (i.e., flood, earthquake, etc.) or have happy endings." They are surprisingly rarely digging for dirt.

- Almost always, "something that photographs well: kids, helicopters, visible disasters (collapsed buildings post earthquake, etc.) are all good. Action shots always best—i.e., people actually getting vaccinated, actually clearing a road."

- "NO JARGON. Say something like 'capacity building' and watch them tune out."

- "Pithy quotes that non-development people can understand."

- "Some emoting if appropriate ('I've never seen anything like it, etc., etc.')."

- "Some assurance of exclusivity if I sit in some NGO's 4x4 for eight brutal hours to cover something."

- "Public Information Officers who don't oversell a story—gimme the straight dope and we can have a relationship/burn me once and both you and your agency will become one of the horror stories journos tell each other."

- "No-bullshit backgrounders from people local/ foreign who grok the nuances."

- "Use of a sat-phone in emergencies."

- "Abundant, free comfort food—a foot-rub after a long day in the field, access to liquor and sympathetic, goggle-eyed young women on their first field missions."

- "And finally, someone who can opine on the record about the Scientologist's Emergency Response Unit."

6

ESCAPING THE EXPAT BUBBLE

We are all cultural relativists here—brochettes are no better than burgers, and baseball is no better than buzkashi. (In fact, baseball is deadly boring. Especially compared to a sport that involves playing polo with a dead goat.) Yet even as we pause to admire the wonderful mosaic of world cultures, it's worth remembering that diversity can also be a bitch. We spend our entire youth becoming socialized in our own cultural mores, learning such important lessons as when it's appropriate to look someone in the eyes, what qualifies as hooker clothing, and whether saying ciao is considered unbearably pretentious.

The problem with travel is that it screws with our finely tuned cultural compass. Suddenly, it's disrespectful to look older adults in the eye.

Suddenly, revealing your elbows is a sign of moral depravity. Suddenly, it's alright to say ciao, even if you aren't Italian. Herewith some general advice for navigating different—and at times rather interesting—cultural waters.

Can't We All Just Get Along: Some Very Basic Advice

There are no hard and fast rules—what's acceptable in one country would mark you as a hopeless degenerate in another. That said, there are a few general guidelines:

1. Treat anyone older than fifty with pronounced—if not semi-exaggerated—respect, at least until told otherwise.

2. Wear more conservative clothes than you would otherwise. Granted, no one wants to be mistaken for a missionary. That said, long-dress missionary-chic is sometimes preferable to being propositioned by every man on the street.

3. Don't make the A-OK sign. Stick with thumbs up instead.

4. You might be agnostic, or an atheist. Or Wiccan. All respectable choices. Nonetheless, it's far easier to profess a vague monotheism—especially in places like the Middle East or Sub-Saharan Africa, where religious feelings tend to run high—and leave it at that.

5. On a related note, you might want to keep that Star of David necklace at home when visiting Afghanistan, Algeria, Iran, Iraq, Lebanon, Libya, Pakistan, Saudi Arabia, Somalia, Sudan, and Yemen.

6. Finally, if you are gay, probably best to keep that fact to yourself and a few, select friends. Admitting almost any form of racism or bigotry in public has, over the last few decades, become increasingly unacceptable, sort of like smoking indoors, or wearing fur. Tragically, the expectation that everyone will at least pay lip service to tolerance doesn't hold true when it comes to homosexuality, at least not in large

swathes of Africa and the Middle East.

Bonus Advice: How to Behave in a Pentecostal Church

I went because I'd been invited, but also because I was curious. I mean, as an American from the Northeast with a Catholic background, how often do you get to attend a full-on Pentecostal service, and an Easter sermon at that? I came away from the four-hour event with some important life lessons; if attending said services in the future, remember to:

Smile. Get ready for hours of enthusiastic singing. Bring plenty of water. Also, try not to flinch if and when the preacher begins talking about the dangers of 'gayism' and 'lesbianality.' Do not, at all costs, snicker if the teachings move on to the related dangers of masturbation.

If the pastor begins laying hands on his parishioners, be prepared for the congregation to speak in tongues in unison, for women to fall to the floor in convulsions, and for children to wail. Your instincts will likely be honed to interpret babbling, convulsing, and wailing as signs that something has gone wrong. Do not react. Do, however, look for an escape route in the event the preacher decides to prove his prowess by laying hands on YOU and infusing the Westerner amongst the congregation with the power of the Holy Spirit.

(I chose to scoop up the wailing child sitting beside me and hold her in front of me as a sort of human shield. This proved a good choice; it deterred the preacher without forcing me to flee for the nearest exit in what would have been an embarrassing—and no doubt insulting—rush.) (L.G.)

Understanding Hand Gestures; Or Knowing When to Run

A-OK sign

You may think that making the A-OK sign is acceptable. You may believe that sometimes the A-OK sign sums up your feelings better than anything else. You may have been making the

A-OK sign all your life (in which case, you're probably American). Now is really the time to stop. Unless, of course, you want your conversational interlocutor to think that you like flashing the international sign for vagina in the middle of your conversations. In that case, flash away.

Thumbs up

Always in good taste. Except in Iran. Or Afghanistan.

Right hand over the heart, a serious-thoughtful-slightly regretful look on your face

This is perfect for (a) turning down an overly incessant street vendor, or (b) trying to get through a conversation about religion without actually expressing any of your own beliefs. Glancing upwards occasionally also helps—in both circumstances.

Pointing

Pointing, especially at people, is often considered

rude. Then again, sometimes it's useful to point. Like when there's a fire.

Waving your arms and screaming

Depending on the circumstances, this might also be appropriate—say, when trying to escape a riot.

The line between exuberance and impending violence

It's hard to tell when someone crosses the line between exuberant, animated hand gestures as part of a normal conversation, and exuberant, animated hand gestures that signal impending violence. To that end, the following are probably signs that it's time to wrap up the conversation, or at least begin nodding thoughtfully and backing away slowly:

1. Any time someone appears to point to you.

2. Any time someone appears to point to you repeatedly.

3. Any time someone begins jabbing you with his or her finger.

4. Any time someone reaches for a firearm.

Everything else should be fine. (Keep in mind that numbers one through three are all considered a necessary part of polite conversation in Israel.)

How to Realize When Someone Is Hitting on You

Generally, blatant expressions indicating an interest in getting to know you better are a sure sign you're being hit on. Be especially wary of people asking if they can "be your friend." If they're not hitting on you, chances are they're going to ask you for something. But probably they're hitting on you *and* are also going to wind up asking for something. The appropriate response is to smile politely and turn away. If you're not able to—say, for example, the person in question is a high-ranking member of the national parliament—a bland response along the lines of, "well of course, we're already friends. I look forward to working with you," can usually diffuse the situation.

The difficulty arises when things get a little

more opaque. In Togo, for example, a pretty common pickup line is, "I'd like to know your house." "House" of course being a euphemism for something a little more personal. In these situations it's probably wise to assume a dirty connotation, then naïvely chalk the confusion up to your novice-level French.

Bonus Advice: How to Interpret a Dirty Look at a Bar

The open air bar was exceptionally crowded. It was, after all, one of the few dry Fridays in the middle of Liberia's rainy season, and everyone who'd been cooped up indoors was out celebrating the brief dry spell. You could barely stand without being jostled, and it just wasn't my fault that the crowd had me pushing up against the woman seated on a bar stool behind me. Unfortunately, that didn't stop her from giving me dirty looks, which, after a while, started to annoy me.

When she left the seat to wander off, I hopped onto the stool myself to make more room in the

crowd and get off my feet. When she came back
sometime later, I was irritated enough from our
previous interaction not to return the stool. She
began leaning into me more than the crowd
necessitated, and I thought, perhaps, that we'd
begun a Bitch Battle for the Bar Stool. Refusing to
be cowed, I pushed back thinking, "Listen, sister,
you left, and that's what happens. Back off. The
chair's mine." After a few minutes of this, she
looked at me, batted her eyes, and said, "I like the
way you rub."

Not what I'd been expecting, to say the least.
When she then asked, coyly, whether or not we'd
met before, followed by a suggestion that she'd
"seen me around," I realized that I'd misinterpreted
the dirty looks from before. Perhaps they'd still
been "dirty," just of a different variety. (L.G.)

Speaking the Lingo

We all dream dreams of fitting in. We won't. Not
least because most of us will never learn to speak
the language. That said, it is worthwhile to learn a

few phrases in whatever passes for the local patois.
Essential phrases include:

- Yes (French: *Oui*; Spanish: *Sí*)

- No (French: *Non*; Spanish: *No*)

- Please (French: *S'il vous plaît*; Spanish: *Por favor*)

- Thank you (French: *Merci*; Spanish: *Gracias*)

- Are you kidding? (French: *Tu blagues*; Spanish: *Me estás cargando*)

- You are overcharging (French: *C'est trop cher*; Spanish: *Me estás cobrando demasiado*)

- I will pay half that amount (French: *Je vais payer la moitie de cela*; Spanish: *Te voy a dar la mitad*)

- Fuck you (French: *Va te faire foutre*; Spanish: *Vete a la mierda*)

- More beer, please (French: *Encore de la bière, s'il vous plaît*; Spanish: *Más cerveza, por favor*)

- Do you sell cigarettes? (French: *Vous vendez de clopes?*; Spanish: *¿Venden cigarillos acá?*)

- Where's the bathroom? (French: *Où est la toilette?*;

Spanish: *¿Donde está el baño?*)

- I am not a hooker (French: *Je ne suis pas une pute*; Spanish: *No soy puta*)

  Other useful phrases included:

- I have nothing to declare (French: *Je n'ai rein a declarer*; Spanish: *No tengo nada que declarar*)

- That's a nice weapon (French: *C'est une jolie arme*; Spanish: *Es una linda arma*)

- Of course I love/support the government/your movement (French: *Bien sur j'aime / soutiens le gouvernement / votre movement*; Spanish: *Claro que amo / apoyo el govierno / su movimiento*)

- I have no money (French: *Je n'ai pas d'argent*; Spanish: *No tengo plata*)

- I don't have any more money (French: *Je n'ai plus argent*; Spanish: *No tengo más plata*)

- Nice shooting, officer (French: *Bonne fusillade, officier*; Spanish: *Buen tiro, oficial*)

- Death to the imperialist / capitalist / Western dogs! (French: *Mort aux chiens impérialistes /*

capitalistes / occidentaux!; Spanish: *¡Muerte a los perros imperialistas / capitalistas / occidentales!*)

- Please, take the vehicle (French: *S'il vois plaît, prenez le vehicule*; Spanish: *Por favor, tomen el vehiculo*)

- Is that meat? (French: *C'est de la viande?*; Spanish: *¿Eso es carne?*)

- Thank you, I really couldn't eat any more chicken / fish / goat / lamb (French: *Merci, je ne peux plus manger du poulet / poisson / chevre / agneau*; Spanish: *No puedo comer más pollo / pescado / chivito / cordero*)

- Has this water been filtered? (French: *Cette eau, elle est filtrée?*; Spanish: *¿Es agua filtrada?*)

- I'm here to help (French: *Je suis la pour aider*; Spanish: *Estoy aquí para ayudar*)

- No, really (French: *No, vraiment*; Spanish: *No, de verdad*)

- I have no other agenda (French: *Je n'ai pas d'agenda cachée*; Spanish: *No tengo otro propósito*)

- No, of course I'm not Buddhist / Christian / Hindu / Jewish / Muslim (French: *No, bien sure je* ne suis pas bouddhiste / chrétienne / hindoue / juive / musulmane; Spanish: *No, claro quo no soy budista / cristiano / hindú / judío / musulmán*)

- Is there malaria in this area? (French: *Il ya de la malaria ici?*; Spanish: *¿Hay malaria aquí?*)

- Do you have a mosquito net I could use? (French: *Vous avez un moustiquaire que je pourrais utiliser*; Spanish: *¿Tienen un mosquitero que pueda usar?*)

- I saw a crocodile / scorpion / snake in my room (French: *J'a vu un crocodile / scorpion / serpent dans ma chambre*; Spanish: *Vi un cocodrilo / escorpión / una serpiente en mi cuarto*)

- What should I do? (French: *Qu'est-ce que je devrais faire?*; Spanish: *¿Qué tengo que hacer?*)

- Does anyone have a spare battery for my phone? (French: *Est-ce que quelqu'un a une batterie de rechange pour mon téléphone?*; Spanish: *¿Alguien tiene una pila extra para mi telefono?*)

- I can pay (French: *Je peux payer*; Spanish: *Puedo pagar*)

Bonus Advice: How Not to Order Goat Brochettes

Of course, sometimes the only thing worse than not speaking the local language at all is trying to speak it in the first place. I was eating with colleagues in Burundi one night, and it was taking forever for the goat brochettes to arrive.

Which was frustrating, seeing as how (a) goat brochettes were the only thing on the menu, so the kitchen didn't have all that much to juggle, and (b) goat brochettes aren't particularly complicated to make—cut goat, put on skewer, put skewer on grill, serve.

After an hour or so, I leaned over to the colleague on my right and said, in French, "I'm hungry." Which, granted, is not a particularly interesting conversational gambit, but was all I could think to say at the moment. Besides, he'd been making an effort to speak in English, and I wanted to show off my French.

Unfortunately, due to some ironic twists in the French language, the word for hunger sounds similar to the word for woman; or at least it does with my accent. Further, you're supposed to say, "I have hunger," instead of "I am hungry." The upshot of these various vocabulary and grammatical mistakes was that I announced, "I am a woman."

He had the good graces to look slightly surprised, seeing as how I am not, in fact, a woman. Seeing his reaction, I thought he simply hadn't heard. So I said the same, but much, much louder. At which point all conversation in the restaurant came to a sudden halt.

It was only later that I wondered why my colleague only seemed slightly surprised. (M.B.)

7

DEALING WITH WARS, REBELLIONS, AND OTHER EXCITING EVENTS

The realization that you've wandered into the middle of a firefight or a minefield might cause a fair bit of anguish. It might also cause you to question any number of life choices, especially given that most of your high school and college classmates at home are safely ensconced in their cubicles and offices, drinking coffee, and checking email.

Of course, that vision of cubicles might be the exact reason you chose to live in conflict zones in the first place. Actually dying, however, tends to have a detrimental effect on your sense of moral superiority.

Whose Side Are You On?

Neither side. Oh, you might have preferences, biases, a strong rooting interest. You might feel a strong sense of solidarity. That's all well and good. Yet there's a tremendous difference between feeling such and actually acting on it. Most expat jobs in conflict-prone countries—aid workers, journalists and the like—require at least the appearance of neutrality, if only to allow you to work with both the government and any rebel groups you might come across.

Wearing your heart on your sleeve tends to limit such options. It also puts you at risk, as neutrality (as well as independence and impartiality) is traditionally the best way to guarantee some modicum of security.

Of course, that's all rather theoretical. When confronted by the secret police or an upset looking rebel commander, feel free to proclaim your undying and unwavering support for whichever side is currently threatening you with weapons or holding you incommunicado.

To that end, it's useful to learn how to say both "good shooting, officer," and "the police are Western dogs" in the local language (see above).

What a Rebel Group's Name Says about Its Temperament

Perhaps you find yourself in a country that is currently trying to resolve some sort of political impasse through the ever-expedient means of ethnic cleansing. In such situations, crosscultural understanding is more important than ever, especially when you're trying to translate the names of various liberation fronts from one language to another.

The basic rule to keep in mind is that rebel group names are meant to attract attention from certain (hopefully wealthy and/or easily conscriptable) constituencies. Names are, at the end of the day, part of a broader branding and fundraising campaign.

Any armed group that mentions Islam in its name will have a difficult time attracting support from the West, while any group that calls itself democratic probably shouldn't go to the trouble of opening a fundraising office in the Gulf States.

When trying to decode what a rebel group's name actually means, a few additional rules also come in handy:

1. Any group that proclaims itself to be democratic most certainly isn't.

2. Ditto any group that goes to the trouble of calling itself united, seeing as how most are either a splinter faction of some earlier movement, or on the verge of self-imploding.

3. Any group that mentions some variation of God or the Lord in its name probably doesn't practice any version of religion likely to be recognized by, say, Jesus, Muhammad, or Buddha. Unless, of course, these religious leaders enjoyed abducting child soldiers in their free time.

4. Any group that identifies itself as a People's Movement was probably named before 1990,

when the chances of attracting the attention and funding of the USSR were considerably higher than they are today. Of course, once named, it's hard to change, branding being what it is.

5. Beware groups with names that aren't easily reduced to friendly sounding acronyms, such as the Taliban ("religious students") in Afghanistan or the Shabab ("young men") in Somalia.

6. Finally, any group calling itself MILF—as do our friends in the Moro Islamic Liberation Front—probably doesn't have a finely developed sense of irony. Proceed accordingly.

Naming Your Own Rebel Group

If you don't know—or can't be bothered to learn— the name of any local rebel groups, then use the handy rebel name generator below. Simply choose at least one name from each of the following categories (you can play with the order too, if you're feeling creative), then acronymize accordingly:

Who you are: Country name / regional name / ethnic group

What you believe: Democratic / Islamic / People's

What you want: Equality / Freedom / Justice / Liberation / Revolutionary / Unity

How you'll organize to achieve your goals: Army / Congress / Front / Movement / Party

Bonus Arabic version—The word Hizbi means party. And, really, you can't go wrong with Hizbi Islami. Because if there isn't already an Islamic Party that disagrees with the state, there probably should be. (Also works well in non-Arab Muslim countries, like Afghanistan and Pakistan.)

Bonus French version—Just say Forces Unies et Démocratiques. Because every country needs a rebel group called FUD.

Bonus Spanish version—Invent a local offshoot of either FARC or Sendero Luminoso. Easier still, invent a local cartel.

What to Do When You Hear Gunfire

Duck. If no one else around you is panicking, then very calmly resume whatever you were doing, and pretend to carry on as though nothing happened.

In case of any confusion, look to see what the local person you know and respect the most is doing (crouching, running, praying), and do the same. They are guaranteed to have a better understanding of the difference between *oh that* and *oh shit* than you are.

If everyone else is, in fact, panicking, then definitely consider panicking. Oftentimes, the only people remaining calm are the ones who don't understand what's going on.

Bonus Advice: What To Do When You Hear a Rocket

Both the sound and the tremor woke me from a deep slumber. I went from groggy to alert in half a heartbeat, however, once I saw the smoke rising above the city, somewhere not too far behind my compound walls, and realized there'd been a blast of some sort nearby. I'd only been in Kabul for three weeks and already an internet café around the corner from my compound had been suicide bombed, an acquaintance had been kidnapped, and colleagues in our Jalalabad office had had to flee the grounds when rioters started ransacking the city. It seemed entirely probable that a bomb had just exploded.

I ran out of my semi-detached room in my employer's guesthouse in my pajamas, uncertain how to respond. Our indolent security guards were still dozing by the front gate, so I went over to investigate.

They seemed very unconcerned about the blast, and told me in bored, sleepy English just to go back to sleep.

There is nothing to be done now, they reasoned. It would be different, maybe, if there had been another blast immediately thereafter, or even sounds of gunfire, but to their experienced ears, this had been an isolated event, somewhere far enough away, albeit only about six blocks, not to warrant a break from their slumber.

I had a hard time following their advice, adrenaline being a stimulant and all, but eventually managed to fall back asleep. The next day rumors had it that a generator in the nearby hospital had exploded all on its own, the result of poor maintenance, not militant intentions. (L.G.)

How to Avoid Minefields: When Not to Take the Path Less Traveled

The best way to survive a minefield is not to enter one in the first place. Minefields not only tend to remain long after the conflict has ended, but mines also have a disturbing habit of migrating as rains wash away soil and the landscape changes.

And, just to make things more interesting, mines aren't only in the ground—they can also be placed in trees and bushes.

1. The best thing to do is to ask the locals, who've probably developed a rather Darwinian knowledge of where it's safe and unsafe to tread. Even if you're not in a country that was heavily mined, it's best to never, ever, go picnicking

or hiking without double-checking that the surrounding terrain is clear of the remnants of war. Stepping on an explosive device is just not the way you want to end your spontaneous day off.

2. It's also a good idea to stay on well-marked roads and paths.

3. Avoid any place marked with a red or orange sign that includes the words "mine" or "danger," the picture of a mine, or a skull and crossbones—which should, by the way, be fairly obvious advice.

4. Also avoid any area marked off with ribbons or rocks painted red, piles of stones, flags in the ground, or grass tied together. Conversely, a line of small rocks painted white often marks an area cleared by your friendly neighborhood deminers.

5. UXO means unexploded ordnance. If you're an explosives ordnance disposal expert, the difference between a mine and unexploded

ordinance can be fascinating. For anyone else, the effect is pretty much the same. In short, if you find something that looks like it might explode, or was designed to explode, definitely don't touch, don't move, and call loudly for help.

How to Deal with the Police

Police in some less developed countries are likely to ask for bribes. When this happens, the thing to remember is that this is, fundamentally, a negotiation, mostly based on a sliding scale between (a) how much trouble they can cause you, and (b) how willing you are to pay. As with any negotiation, it's best to remain calm.

Sometimes you'll pay, and sometimes you won't. There's really no rhyme or reason to it. Depends mostly on your mood. And theirs. That said, here are some basic tips for negotiating with the police:

1. Don't grovel.

2. Unless, of course, they're pointing a gun at you. Then grovel all you want.

3. Remain confident but polite.

4. Don't make threats. Especially when you know—and, more importantly, they know—that it's an empty threat. The only thing worse than a bored policeman out to make a little money is a bored, angry policeman who's convinced that you've just challenged his manhood.

5. At least, don't make threats that you can't back up. Don't say you're going to call your ambassador unless you actually have the ambassador on speed-dial.

6. Remember that the police need to save face—especially in front of a crowd.

7. They want money, but they don't necessarily want aggravation. Police will usually steer away from any course of action that involves them filling out paperwork. Which is useful to remember if someone is threatening to arrest you over a relatively minor offense.

8. Of course, this only applies in countries where

the police actually have to fill out paperwork.

9. A corollary to this: agreeing to pay a bribe on the condition that you are given a "receipt" is usually a good way to avoid paying said bribe. This works especially well if the bribe has been presented to you as a "fine" for some trumped up transgression.

10. If you've actually broken the law, your room to maneuver is significantly less than it would be otherwise.

11. Try to talk about football. (Not American football, silly. The other football.) Just remember: everyone, even the police, loves Manchester United or Real Madrid. You should too. Unless they like Arsenal or Barcelona, in which case you're screwed.

Bonus Advice: Getting Arrested for Public Urination

I never thought I would get arrested for public urination in northern Kenya. (A charge, I might add, that was completely unjustified, seeing as how I'd taken the time to go behind the shipping container before relieving myself.) Instead of paying the requisite bribe, however, I took out my notebook, slammed it on the desk of the small police station, and demanded the policemen's names, threatening to call the UN. Which might have been the single dumbest thing I've ever said.

The UN does many things. Sending a squad of peacekeepers to rescue random aid workers accused of public urination is not one of them. I might as well have threatened to call the League of Nations. Or, for that matter, the Justice League.

The two policemen stared at me in shock—mostly, shock that I could be so stupid. I began to blush. And then they began yelling. An hour of yelling, mostly variations on the theme of, "who the fuck do you think you are/how dare you threaten us/it's going to be our particular joy and amusement to throw you into a Kenyan prison." Realizing the error of my ways, I quickly downshifted from bluster to contrition to outright begging to silence. Which eventually did the trick, as they grew bored of yelling and finally just let me go.

Needless to say, getting arrested again fifteen minutes later for smoking in a non-smoking area at the airport didn't greatly improve the situation. (M.B.)

How to Deal with People Begging for Money

You're sitting in a taxi on a brutally crowded street. Traffic isn't moving at all. Your window is rolled up, to keep out the dust, or the noise, or to keep someone from reaching in and trying to grab your bag. Young men walk down the rows of cars, hawking everything from fake soccer jerseys to umbrellas to car mats. Behind them comes a young, emaciated woman in old, tattered clothes, carrying a baby. Maybe the child looks hungry. She knocks on the window, holding out her hand—the universal sign asking for money.

Or maybe it's a seven-year-old child at the window, carrying a younger sibling.

You have small change—depending on the local currency and the conversion rates, it equates to a few cents, or at most a dollar; it's also enough to buy a meal, or at least some food. What do you do?

The moral calculus is about as straightforward as it gets—here's someone clearly in need; the crumpled bills that you think are almost worthless are, for her, the difference between feeding her child or not. You roll down the window, and hand over the money. She smiles to say thank you, and moves on to the next car.

Which is where the story should end. Instead, another woman holding a baby immediately comes up, before you've had a chance to roll the window up. Three more young children suddenly appear, all holding out their hands. You've given to the other woman, why won't you give to us? Their need is just as great.

This doesn't mean that you shouldn't give. You should, however, be aware that giving to one person invariably means a second and a third and a fourth will ask as well.

Bonus Advice: Entertaining a Playboy Playmate in Afghanistan

I once worked for an aid agency that—for reasons lost to logic and the need to raise funds—decided to send a celebrity delegation to visit our country office in Afghanistan. The delegation included a German TV personality, a little known German actress whose main claim to fame was that she was once a Playboy Playmate.

Part of me was appalled—cultural sensitivity and all the rest—and part of me was thrilled. Absolutely thrilled. Needless to say, I completely failed to get her attention over the first few days of her visit. Undaunted, I decided to try and make an impression when the delegation visited a widows' feeding program that my agency ran in a particularly destitute district of Kabul. The distribution site was out beyond the edge of nowhere, an urban wasteland of destroyed, bombed out buildings and hard, frozen mud. Over a hundred and fifty widows in blue burkhas milled around in front of an abandoned, graffitied apartment building. Children ran through the crowd.

As we stood around, waiting for the distribution to begin, I couldn't stop staring at the kids, bundled against the cold in old clothes and jackets and rags. I saw a child selling candy, and on a whim decided to buy all the candy and hand it out for free— visions of a tall, Jewish Santa Claus danced in my head, mixed with hopes that this might just win the Playmate's attention and admiration.

I paid the child the equivalent of three dollars for his entire carton of candy, and handed out the first piece. There was a moment of beatific calm, and then a wild scrum erupted—kids coming in from all over, pushing over each other, fighting to reach the carton. I belatedly realized that street urchins would not, in fact, spontaneously form a line when confronted with free candy. I stood there, stunned for a moment, and then a particularly enterprising child hit the carton from underneath, sending candy flying everywhere.

Pandemonium. A wild, sprawling mob of kids kicking and pushing and screaming for candy, while Gulliver-like I stood shocked above the fray.

In an attempt to impose a little order I held the box above my head and yelled—in English, and hence in vain—for everyone to settle down. Unfortunately, I can't do two things at once, so as I screamed I also inadvertently lowered the box, at which point another child hit it from underneath, knocking the rest of the candy into the air. All hell truly broke loose—kids fighting each other for the candy, and in the distance I saw a widow knocked to the ground. (The limited visibility offered by a burkha being a definite drawback in a melee.)

I had another moment to savor the clusterfuck I'd created before an energetic eight-year-old took out my knees. I went down like a stone, children stepping on my chest, on my face in the mad rush for candy. At which point what little instinct I possess took over, and I grabbed at kids, trying to use them to lever myself back up.

A few seconds later I was dragged to freedom by one of our drivers.

Needless to say, the Playmate was not impressed.

It took me years longer to realize the true moral

of the story—well, beyond the rather obvious "don't be a schmuck." When confronted with those in need, it's a natural human instinct to help, or to try and help, whether motivated by the most elevated or self-interested of reasons. Yet trying to help without a sense of what you're doing will—more often than not—make things worse.

Unintended consequences are a bitch. Yet if we live in hard and sometimes horrible places, the least we can do is try and not make things worse. (M.B.)

Dealing with Stress

Any number of people will talk about the ways in which you should deal with stress. Exercise. Healthy living. Meditation. Keeping perspective.

Which is all very well and true, but most of us aren't quite that disciplined. Especially when you're living in a foreign country, and even more when you're in a not-very-pleasant part of a foreign country. Like, say, working in a refugee camp. Or living in a capital city with only infrequent electricity and hot water. Or slowly getting used to the sound of mortars, rockets, and gunfire.

In those situations, you're much more likely to deal with stress by drinking, smoking, becoming increasingly cynical or emotionally removed, losing your temper with increasing frequency, and/or fucking everything that moves. Not that these are healthy, but they are normal, insofar as normal can be defined as "doing what everyone else is doing."

Keeping this in mind, a few thoughts. First, use protection. Really, you don't want to come home from Afghanistan/Congo/Zimbabwe with a child. Or an STD.

Second, and equally important, the issue isn't drinking or smoking or sleeping around *per se*. It's realizing when these coping mechanisms are beginning to fuck with the rest of your life. Which is, granted, a fairly self-evident thing to say, but also a wee bit difficult to realize when you're the one drinking and smoking and hitting on the semi-attractive aid worker who just arrived last week.

A few signs that it might be time to leave, or at

least go on an extended R&R:

1. When the drinking begins to interfere with your ability to do your job. Say, if you're often still drunk when you show up to work in the mornings.

2. Needless to say, drinking at work is not a good sign.

3. When you realize that you're losing your temper—really losing your temper, screaming and yelling—more than, say, once a week.

4. Any time someone mentions your name and "aneurysm" in the same sentence, it's probably best to re-evaluate your coping mechanisms.

5. When you find it impossible to relax or unwind, even when hanging out with friends.

6. Or, worse, when you find it impossible to relax or unwind, even when drunk or high.

7. When people you work or drink with begin pulling you aside and mentioning that they're worried or concerned, or when you overhear

someone mentioning that you don't look quite right anymore. Especially when the people doing the worrying are barely functional alcoholics themselves.

8. Especially if you respond by yelling at said people.

9. When you find yourself taking risks that you would never have taken before. Because you just don't care.

10. When you can see horrible things, and you just don't feel anything at all.

CONCLUSION

TEN SIGNS YOU'VE BEEN OVERSEAS TOO LONG

1. If asked to rank the most wonderful inventions in human history, you would list air conditioning significantly above penicillin, movable type, and the wheel.

2. You're inordinately impressed by working traffic lights. And paved roads.

3. At your leaving party, you jokingly insist that you won't miss the open sewage trenches along the sides of the roads. But you know that you will.

4. In any debate about copyright infringement, you come down firmly on the pro-piracy side. Unless you're talking about the bastards who simply smuggle a videocamera into a movie theater and then market the resulting product

as a clean copy. They can burn in hell.

5. You've developed a Landcruiser fetish.

6. You've also developed an inappropriate, twit-
   ching reaction to fireworks.

7. Doctors at home are slightly intimidated
   by your ability to diagnose various tropical
   diseases.

8. You simply assume that everyone knows
   where Yambio or Ouagadougou are. You
   also think acronyms like NCP, CPA, FDLR,
   AMISOM or ISAF are completely self-
   explanatory.

9. When pregnant friends at home talk about
   getting ready for the hospital, you mentally
   translate "baby bag" into "quick-run" bag.

10. You've worn exactly three pairs of pants and
    four shirts over the past month. Though you do
    take care to mix the combinations according
    to a semi-complex rotating schedule known to
    you and you alone.

Also from Nortia Press

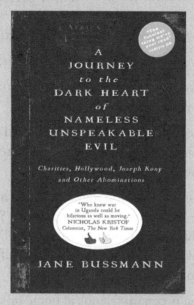

"Who knew war in Uganda could be hilarious
as well as moving."
—Nicholas Kristof, *The New York Times*

"So funny you almost feel guilty laughing."
—Reuters

"Very funny. Jane's got a death wish."
—Matt Stone, *South Park*